THE FABER EASY-PLAY KEYBOARD SERIES

Play
MERRIE ENGLAND

arranged for easy keyboard
by Daniel Scott

FABER MUSIC

Contents

© 1989 by Faber Music Ltd
First published in 1989 by Faber Music Ltd
3 Queen Square, London WC1N 3AU
Music drawn by Sambo Music Engraving
Cover design and typography by John Bury
Printed in England

Trumpet Tune

HENRY PURCELL

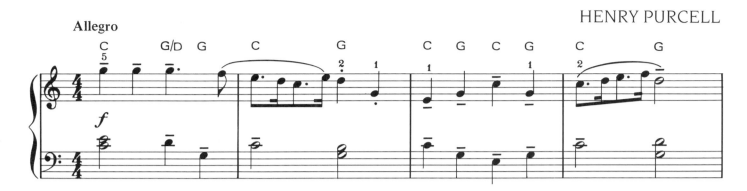

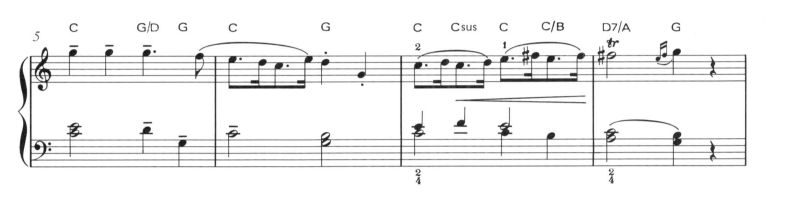

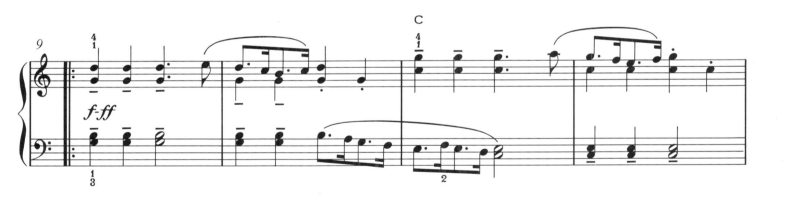

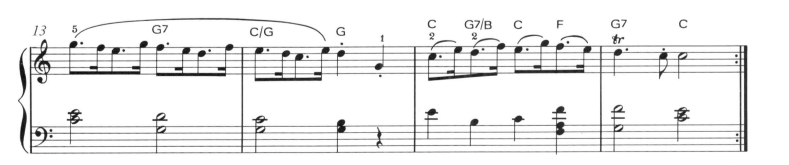

Greensleeves

ANON.

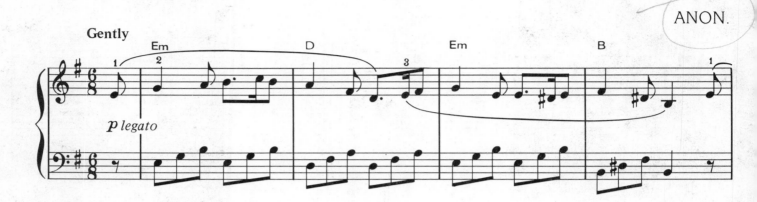

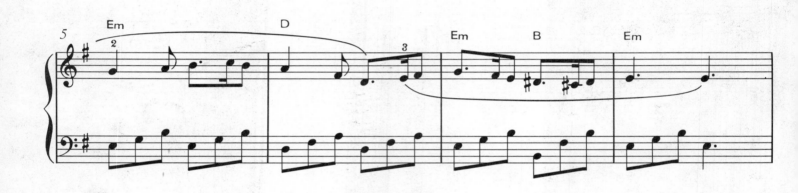

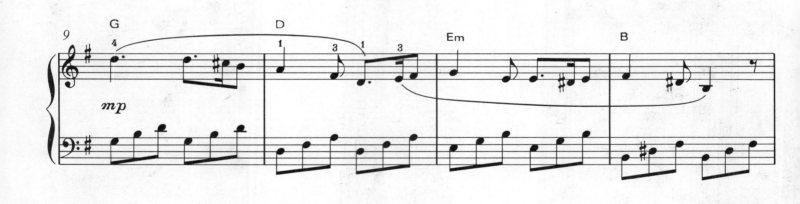

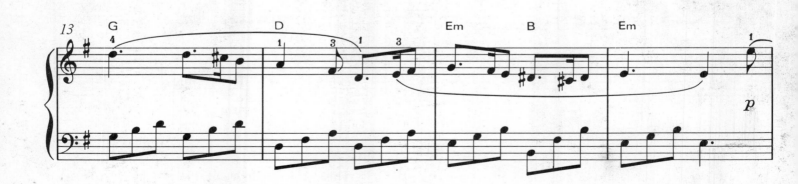

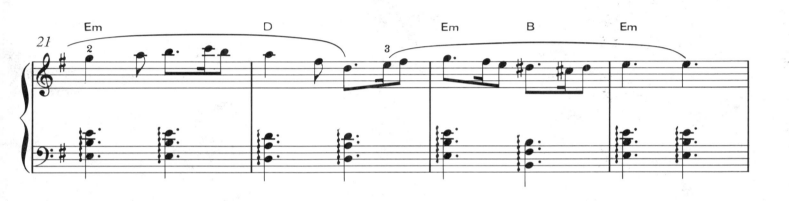

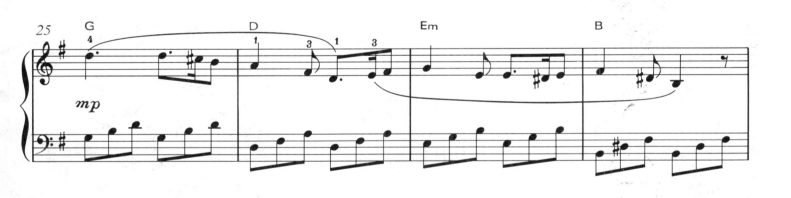

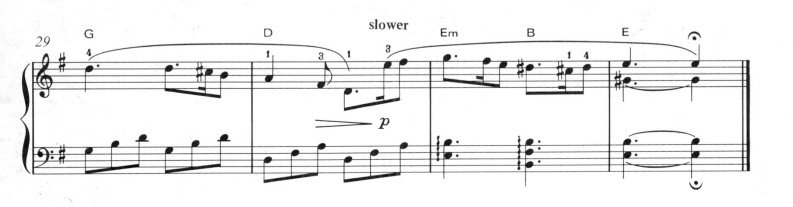

4

The Prince of Denmark's March

JEREMIAH CLARKE

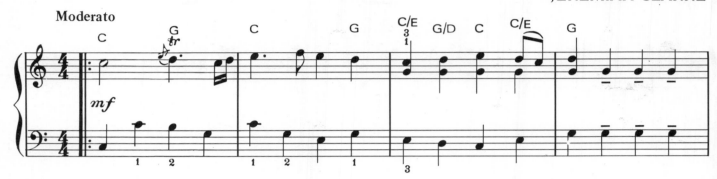

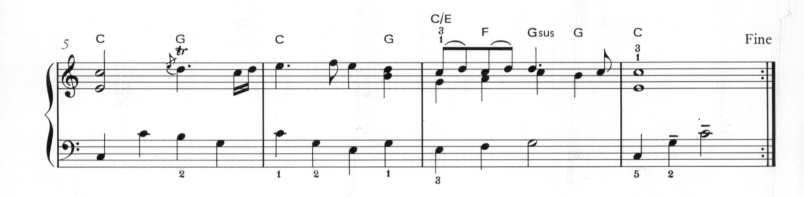

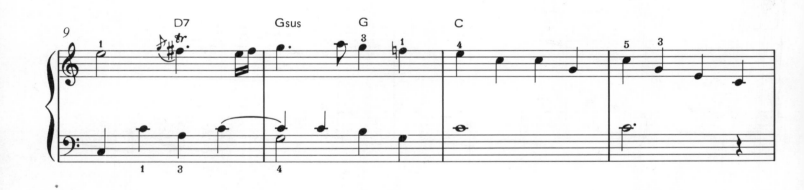

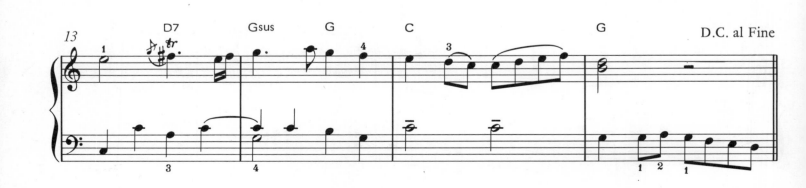

Rule Britannia

THOMAS ARNE

The Arrival of the Queen of Sheba

GEORGE FREDERIC HANDEL

The Harmonious Blacksmith

GEORGE FREDERIC HANDEL

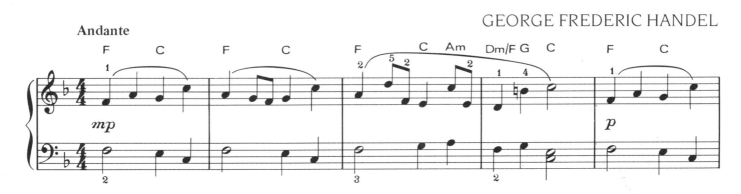

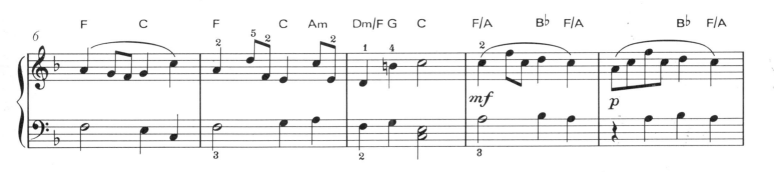

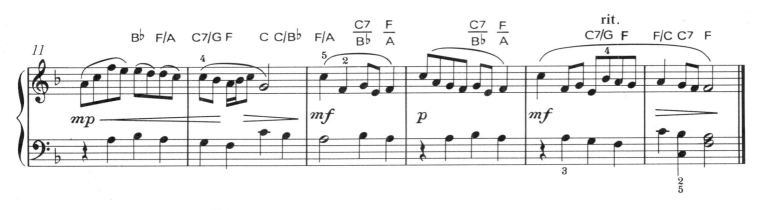

Dead March (*Saul*)

GEORGE FREDERIC HANDEL

9

I know that my Redeemer Liveth (*Messiah*)

GEORG FREDERIC HANDEL

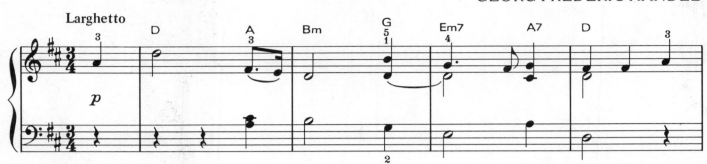

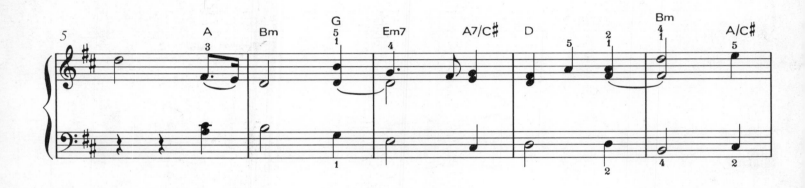

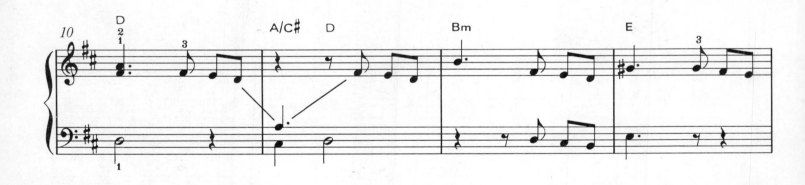

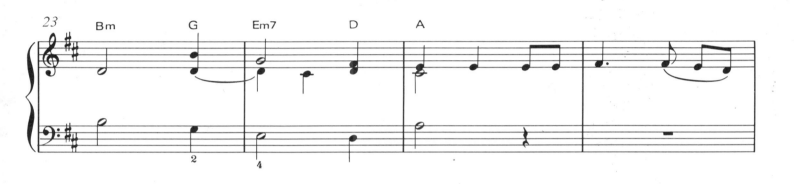

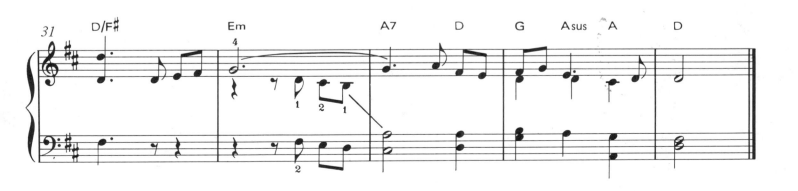

Hallelujah Chorus (*Messiah*)

GEORGE FREDERIC HANDEL

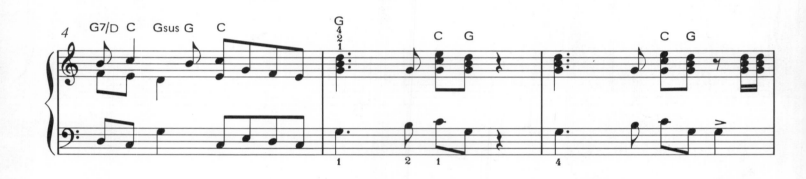

Minuet (*Berenice*)

GEORGE FREDERIC HANDEL

Largo (*Xerxes*)

GEORGE FREDERIC HANDEL

Alla danza (Water Music)

GEORGE FREDERIC HANDEL

See the Conquering Hero Comes

GEORGE FREDERIC HANDEL

Floral Dance

TRAD.

Sailors' Hornpipe

TRAD.

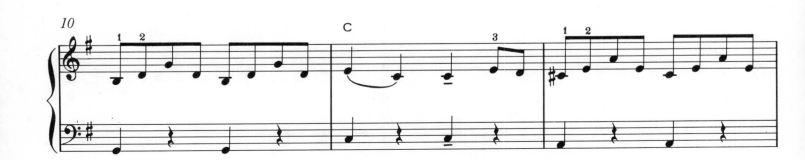

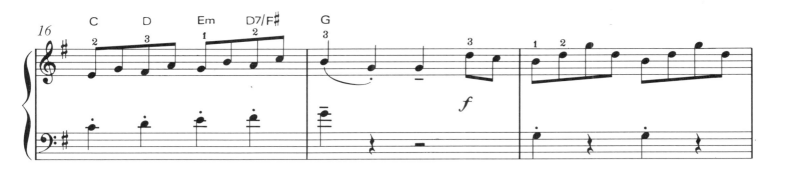

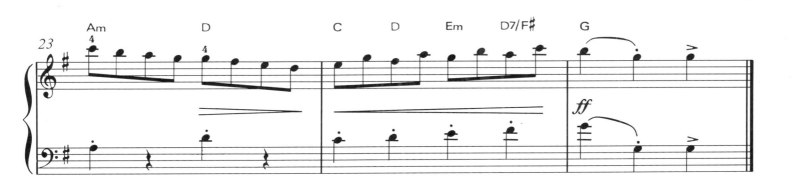

Scarborough Fair

TRAD.

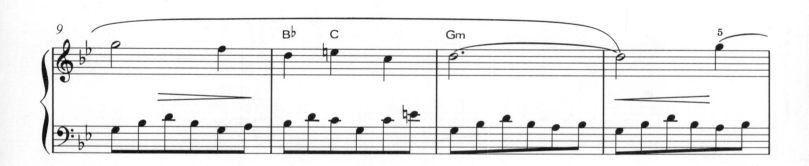

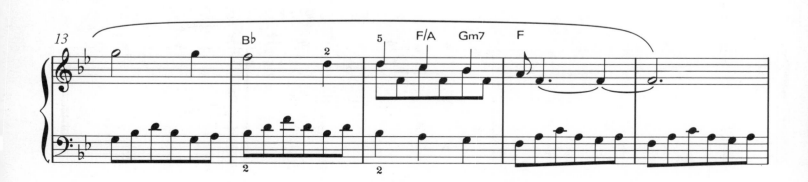

I have a Song to Sing (*The Yeomen of the Guard*)

ARTHUR SULLIVAN

The Sun and I (*The Mikado*)

ARTHUR SULLIVAN

Amazing Grace

TRAD.

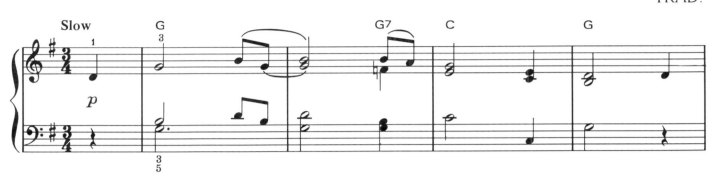

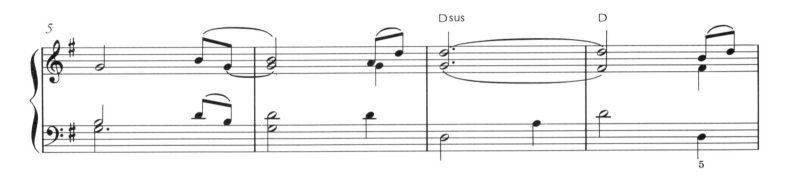

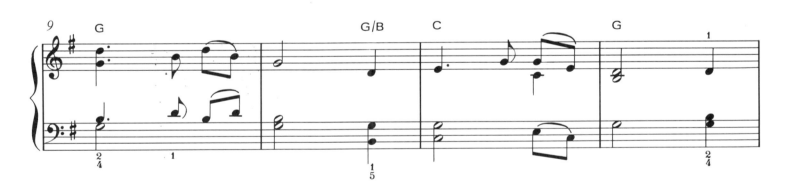

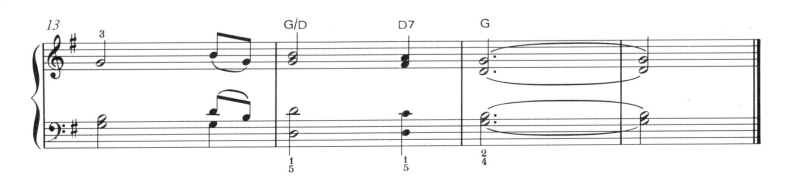

Jerusalem

CHARLES HUBERT PARRY

Nimrod ('Enigma' Variations)

EDWARD ELGAR

Salut d'amour

EDWARD ELGAR

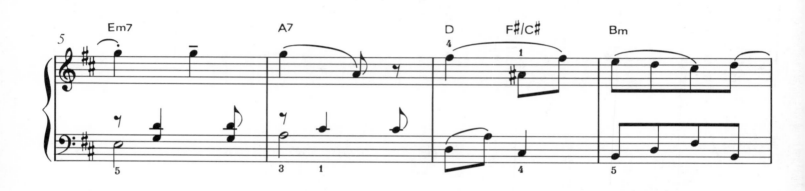

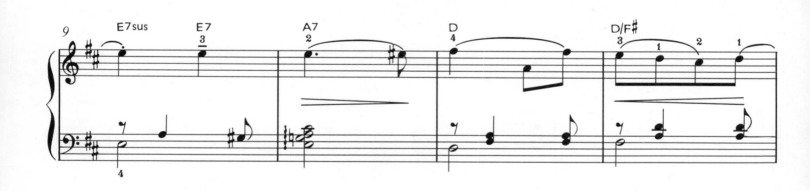

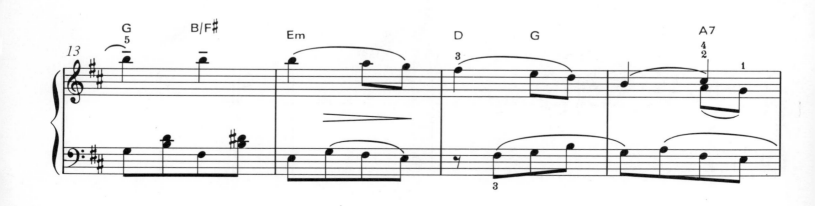

Theme from Symphony No. 1

EDWARD ELGAR

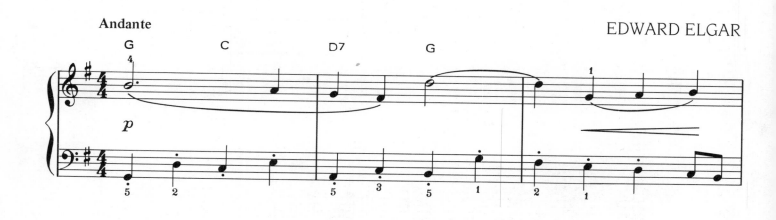

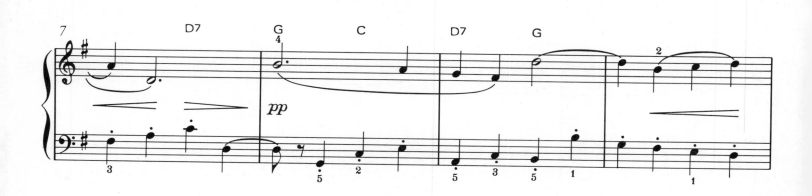

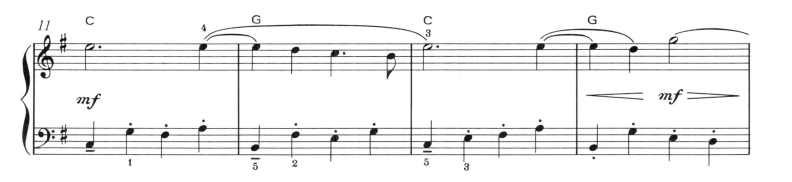

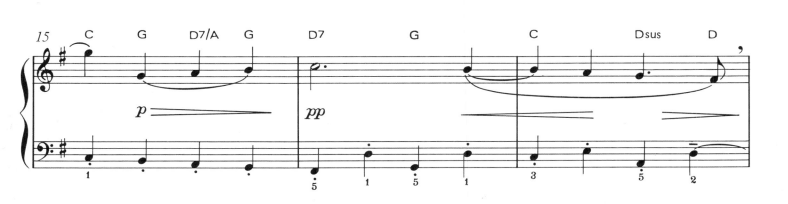

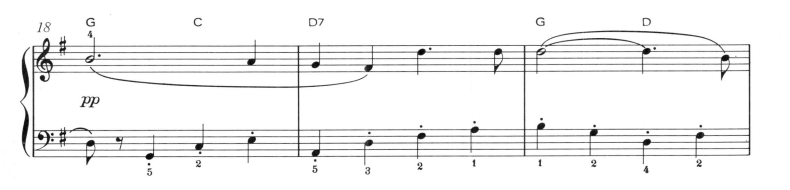

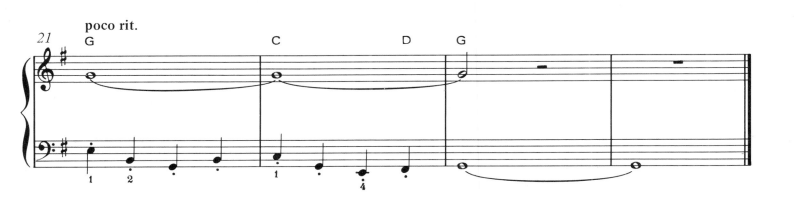

Theme from Cello Concerto

EDWARD ELGAR

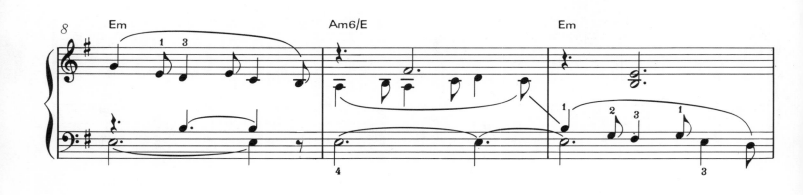

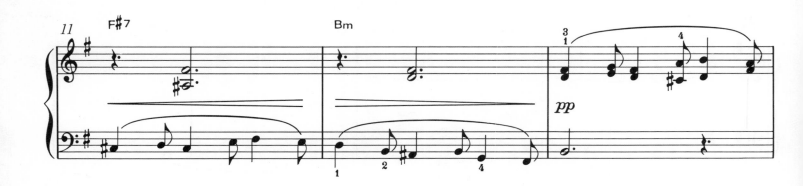